W9-BKE-228

TEEN
SELF-INJURY

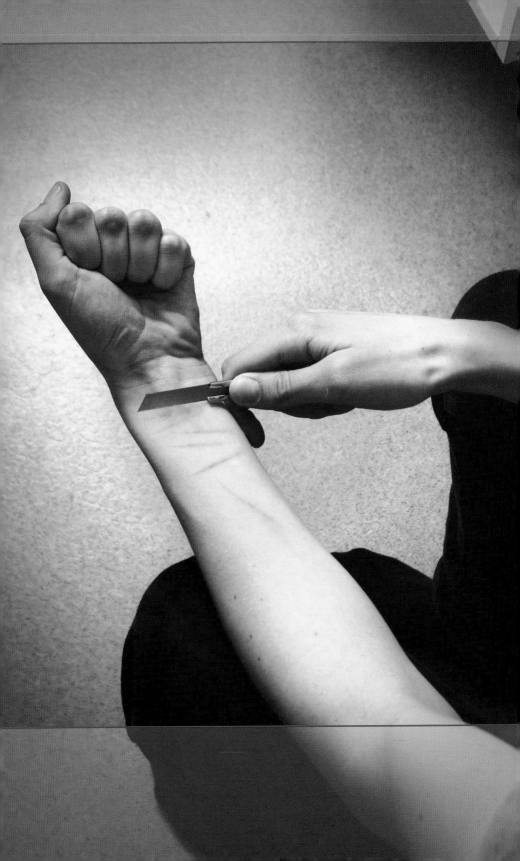

TEEN
SELF-INJURY

BY MELISSA HIGGINS

CONTENT CONSULTANT
SARAH FEUERBACHER, PHD, LCSW-S
CLINIC DIRECTOR
SMU CENTER FOR FAMILY COUNSELING

Essential Library
An Imprint of Abdo Publishing | www.abdopublishing.com

www.abdopublishing.com

Published by Abdo Publishing, a division of ABDO, PO Box 398166, Minneapolis, Minnesota 55439. Copyright © 2015 by Abdo Consulting Group, Inc. International copyrights reserved in all countries. No part of this book may be reproduced in any form without written permission from the publisher. Essential Library™ is a trademark and logo of Abdo Publishing.

Printed in the United States of America, North Mankato, Minnesota
032014
092014

THIS BOOK CONTAINS
RECYCLED MATERIALS

Cover Photo: Mikael Damkier/Shutterstock Images
Interior Photos: Mikael Damkier/Shutterstock Images, 2, 66; Jim Bourdier/AP Images, 6; Shutterstock Images, 10, 95; James A Boardman/Shutterstock Images, 12; Artem Furman/Thinkstock, 16; Thinkstock, 21, 56, 64, 84, 87; Tan Kian Khoon/Thinkstock, 26; Ferdinand Schmutzer, 30; Heike Kampe/Thinkstock, 32; Simon Zupan/Thinkstock, 36; Michael Jung/Shutterstock Images, 39; Tadeusz Ibrom/Shutterstock Images, 44; Wong Chee Yen/Thinkstock, 46; Olga Sapegina/Shutterstock Images, 49; LuminaStock/ Thinkstock, 54; Charles Sykes/Invision/AP Images, 60; The Hollywood Reporter/AP Images, 62; iStockphoto, 69; Katarzyna Bialasiewicz/Thinkstock, 74; Monkey Buisness Images/Thinkstock, 77; Robert Chatterson/Thinkstock, 80; Wavebreakmedia Ltd/ Thinkstock, 91

Editor: Jenna Gleisner
Series Designer: Becky Daum

Library of Congress Control Number: 2014932577

Cataloging-in-Publication Data

Higgins, Melissa.
Teen self-injury / Melissa Higgins.
    p. cm. -- (Essential issues)
Includes bibliographical references and index.
ISBN 978-1-62403-423-7
1. Self-injurious behavior--Juvenile literature. 2. Self-mutilation--Juvenile literature.   I. Title.
616.85--dc23

                                                        2014932577

CONTENTS

CHAPTER
ONE

SELF-INJURY: A GROWING TREND

Lady Diana Spencer seemed to have it all—a noble upbringing, the finest education, invitations to the most lavish parties. But things were not as wonderful as they seemed. Diana was a shy child, and her parents divorced when she was six years old. Her father gained custody, and Diana was shuttled between her parents' homes. In 1981, when she was 20 years old, Diana married Charles, Prince of Wales, heir to the British throne. Instantly, Diana was a celebrity—the subject of intense attention from the media, the public, and the royal family. Her life was no longer her own.

Diana's marriage to Charles was an unhappy one. She struggled with depression and used bulimia to cope with the pressures of a difficult life in the spotlight. She also self-injured. Self-injury is the act of purposely hurting one's own body through acts such as cutting, biting, or burning. In the biography *Diana: Her True Story*,

Revelations of Princess Diana's self-injuring behavior shocked the public in the early 1990s.

Diana revealed that while living in Kensington Palace she cut her wrist with a razor blade and lemon slicer. She often threw herself against a glass cabinet. During an argument with her husband she sliced her thighs and wrist with a penknife. Once while on a flight she locked herself in the bathroom and cut her arms.

In a 1995 television interview with the British Broadcasting Corporation (BBC), Diana explained why she injured herself:

> When . . . you feel no one's listening to you, all sorts of things start to happen. For instance, you have so much pain inside yourself that you try and hurt yourself on the outside because you want help. . . . I was actually crying out because I wanted to get better in order to go forward and continue my duty and my role as wife, mother, Princess of Wales.[1]

Diana separated from Prince Charles in 1992, and they divorced in 1996. She died in a car accident in 1997.

A Year of Revelations

The American public was shocked when excerpts of Diana's biography appeared

"Every clinician says [self-injury is] increasing. . . . I've been practicing for 30 years and I think it's gone up dramatically."[2]
—Michael Hollander, the director of a Massachusetts treatment clinic, to Time magazine.

in the June 22, 1992, issue of *People* magazine. It was hard to believe Diana, Princess of Wales, a popular celebrity and adored British Royal, had cut herself. Cutting, or any form of self-injury, was not something the general public knew much about. It was thought to be a symptom of severe mental disability—a behavior found only in therapists' offices and mental institutions. The public recoiled at the thought of it.

Then, a year later in May 1993, actor Johnny Depp talked about the series of scars he'd cut on his forearm with a knife. "My body is a journal in a way," he told a magazine interviewer. "It's like what sailors used to do, where every tattoo meant something, a specific time in your life when you make a mark on yourself, whether you

A SELF-INJURY DIAGNOSIS

In his book *Cutting: Understanding and Overcoming Self-Mutilation*, psychotherapist Steven Levenkron presents these standards for diagnosing self-injury:

- "Recurrent cutting or burning of one's skin.
- A sense of tension present immediately before the act is committed.
- Relaxation, gratification, pleasant feelings, and numbness experienced [along] with the physical pain.
- A sense of shame and fear of social stigma, causing the individual to attempt to hide scars, blood, or other evidence of the acts of self harm."[3]

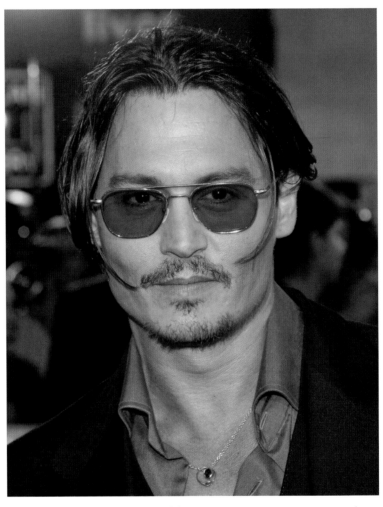

Around the same time as Princess Diana, Johnny Depp also admitted to self-injury.

do it yourself with a knife or with a professional tattoo artist."[4] Again, a stunned public took notice.

In November 1993, an article appeared in *San Francisco Focus* magazine titled "A Bright Red Scream." The article included interviews with a number of young people—noncelebrities without mental health disorders—who cut themselves. Rather than being suicidal acts, these self-injurers reported the practice brought them relief from emotional pain and distress. It was a way to cope—similar to using alcohol or drugs.

Self-injury was nothing new. It had been around for centuries. But this series of revelations from celebrities and noncelebrities alike brought attention to a behavior once thought to be limited to a very small and disturbed portion of the population. As had happened with the eating disorders bulimia and anorexia nervosa decades before, media publicity caused people who self-injured to come forward with their own stories of self-injury. More of them sought help. Researchers and professionals began taking a closer look at what seemed to be a growing phenomenon.

A Growing Practice for Young Adults

For most people, the idea that a cut from a razor blade, scissors, or knife could bring any kind of emotional relief is unthinkable. But the majority of those who self-injure are not mentally disturbed. Rather, they are a growing portion of the population, especially adolescents, unable to cope with the problems in their lives.

Even people who appear to be happy and successful can secretly be self-injuring.

"It's the guy who plays basketball, or normal kids who seem to be doing really well," Dr. Aviva Laye-Gindhu, a self-injury specialist, told an interviewer. "It can be someone who's living an outwardly successful life, but when they take their pants off you see that they have scars running up and down their thighs, and they're hiding a piece of themselves."[5]

Self-injury has been a growing trend since the mid-1990s, and rates of self-injury continue to rise. Some estimates indicate self-injury was three times more prevalent in 2011 than it was in 2007.[6] Reasons for the increase are varied. For some young people, cutting has become something to try because they believe so many others are doing it. Groups of self-injurers who cut themselves encourage others to try it. Internet blogs, websites, chat rooms, and videos devoted to self-injury are only a click away for preteens and teens interested in learning more about it.

Celebrities and the media also drive self-injury. Since the self-injury revelations of Princess Diana and Johnny Depp, several other celebrities have come forward with stories of self-injury. Television shows and movies feature characters who self-injure. Musicians

SELF-INJURY BY THE NUMBERS

According to Mental Health America, approximately 1 percent of the total US population self-injures.[7] The behavior usually begins around puberty and lasts five to ten years. Most people who deliberately injure themselves are adolescents, and they start the practice as young teens. On average, the first time someone self-injures is between 11 and 15 years of age.[8] In one study, researchers found 17 percent of college students self-injured.[9] Another study found up to 8 percent of preadolescents and between 12 to 23 percent of adolescents have purposely harmed themselves at least once.[10] Approximately 60 percent of self-injurers are female, and most people stop the practice as they mature and gain new coping skills.[11]

In New York, self-inflicted injuries are the fifth leading cause of hospitalizations for children aged 10 to 14 years. For 15- to 19-year-olds, self-injury is the second leading cause.[12] Thousands of young adults with self-inflicted injuries visit New York emergency rooms every year.

AN ADDICTION

While some people may find emotional relief in self-injuring, the practice can easily lead to addiction. As Armando Favazza, self-injury expert and professor of psychiatry at the University of Missouri-Columbia, told the *Chicago Tribune*, "This is a pathological form of self-help behavior. When a person is filled with so much anxiety and anger that they feel like they're going to explode, the act of cutting is like lancing a boil, all the bad stuff goes out. Unfortunately, self-mutilation only works for a short period of time . . . so to achieve the same relief, the behavior is repeated."[13]

write songs about self-injury. Even when tales of self-injury are cautionary, some glamour cannot help but attach itself to the practice.

So What's the Problem?

Self-injury can be dangerous. Similar to any drug, it is addictive and can become a difficult habit to break. People may go from injuring themselves once every few months to doing it daily or several times a day. Cutters, for example, may begin making deeper cuts to produce the same "high" they felt when they first started cutting. A cut may become infected or go deeper than planned. Deep gashes can require trips to the emergency room and result in permanent scarring and even death as a result of blood loss.

Another downside of self-injury is emotional. The behavior may initially relieve a person's anxiety, but it does not solve the underlying problem. Instead, the self-injurer adds a feeling of shame and guilt about the wounds on top of the unresolved problem. Adolescence can be a painful passage for almost everyone. As horrendous as self-injury may seem to the general public, for some adolescents, releasing emotional pain with physical pain is how they cope with the pressures of that passage. Is self-injury simply an addiction? A cry for help? Or is it a societal epidemic requiring widespread intervention?

TEENS' DECREASING CAPACITY TO COPE

People who self-injure tend to stop when they find other ways to cope with strong negative feelings. Yet many mental health professionals agree teens have a harder time coping today than ever before. Young people have more stressors than previous generations, such as constant media messages encouraging them to be miniadults. They have more choices to make and are surrounded by more demanding peer groups. Today's teens have a greater sense of loneliness, poorer relationships with parents, and fewer close friends than teens in the past.

CHAPTER
TWO

WHAT IS SELF-INJURY?

To understand self-injury, it's important to know what the behavior is. Self-injury, or self-harm, is also called nonsuicidal self-injury (NSSI). Other names for the practice include self-abuse, self-mutilation, self-injurious behavior, auto-aggression, deliberate self-harm, and parasuicidal behavior. Basically, self-injury is the act of deliberately harming one's own body without the intention of committing suicide.

People most often use self-injury as a way to cope with emotional pain and frustration. Self-injury causes a short period of calm and relief. Then, when the calm and relief wear off, the person is often left with feelings of guilt, shame, and remorse for injuring himself or herself. The painful emotions the self-injurer was trying to get rid of soon return, and the person ends up feeling worse than he or she did before self-injuring. The majority of people who self-injure do it a few times and

Cutting is the most common form of self-injury.

then stop. But for some, the tension felt after an episode of self-injury can lead to another self-injury cycle. It is at this point self-injury becomes a repeated behavior or an addiction.

There are many ways people injure themselves, and a person might use more than one. The most common method of self-injury is cutting—the act of cutting or scratching with a sharp object, such as a knife, needle, scissors, fingernail, razor blade, or

WHY PAIN BRINGS RELIEF

Injuring in order to bring relief sounds a little crazy. After all, humans have survived as a species by staying away from injury and pain. Experts are not exactly sure what happens in the brain of a self-injurer, but biologists generally point to the natural opiate-like endorphins the body releases that dull pain when it is injured. The process is similar to what happens during a "runner's high," when runners feel a sense of euphoria while running long distances. Researchers also credit pain-regulating opiates for why some people cut or burn themselves yet feel no pain. Like all "highs," self-injuring behavior can become addictive. The more often a person self-injures, the more he or she needs and wants to do it again.

Recent studies are also pointing to an interesting connection between physical pain and emotional pain as to why self-injury brings relief. Researchers have found that people with a low threshold for physical pain also have a low threshold for emotional pain. In one study, subjects who were rejected while playing a game also felt more physical pain. And when subjects were given Tylenol they had fewer hurt feelings.[1] The researchers decided the relief people feel after the pain of self-injury raises positive emotions and lowers negative emotions—just as taking pain medication does.

paper clip. One survey found 81 percent of self-injurers reported cutting.[2] But there are many other forms of self-injury, including:

- Biting

- Burning (such as with a lighted match, candle, cigarette, or chemicals)

- Bone breaking

- Carving words or symbols into the skin

- Embedding objects into the skin

- Hair pulling (known as trichotillomania)

- Head banging or head hitting

- Hitting or punching oneself with a fist or object

- Piercing the skin with sharp objects

- Picking at the skin or at scabs so they don't heal

- Pinching

- Poisoning oneself or drinking harmful chemicals

People who self-injure usually harm their wrists, arms, legs, or torso—areas of the body within easy reach that can also be hidden by clothing. But they might injure other parts of the body, such as the head and genitals. Injuries that are only superficial, such as fingernail scratches, may heal and leave no trace. But more serious wounds, such as burns and deep cuts, can leave permanent scars or marks. People usually injure themselves when they are alone rather than when they are in groups.

The Psychology of Self-Injury

Over the years, scientists have come up with different theories to explain why people self-injure. Some psychologists claim the roots of self-injury lie in traumatic childhood experiences, such

Some self-injurers find comfort in pulling out their own hair.

as neglect, sexual abuse, and emotional abuse. After going through these traumas, a person might become angry, depressed, or anxious. If he or she also feels hopeless and has low self-esteem, these feelings could turn into anger and also be directed at oneself. This can lead the person to self-injure as a way to control his or her emotions and feel better. Most psychologists see self-injury as a misguided attempt at self-help.

Dr. Armando Favazza, a cultural psychologist, was the first modern researcher to explore the cultural

CULTURALLY SANCTIONED SELF-INJURY

Even though some types of self-injury would be thought strange if done in Western societies, they are considered normal in the cultures in which they are performed. For example, to make themselves sexually pure, members of a Christian Eastern Orthodox sect practice self-castration. To keep themselves healthy, men in Papua New Guinea make their noses bleed to mimic the female menstrual cycle. To promote social order, teens in many societies go through initiation-rite mutilations, such as getting their skin sliced or their teeth knocked out.

and psychological reasons behind self-injury. Favazza classifies self-injury into two major categories: culturally sanctioned and deviant. Culturally sanctioned self-injury is behavior a society considers normal. For instance, in many Western countries ear piercing and tattoos are culturally sanctioned. In other societies, even severe self-injury might be culturally sanctioned if it is connected with keeping social order or gaining greater spirituality.

Favazza breaks deviant self-injury into three categories: major, stereotypic, and moderate/superficial.

- Major self-injury is rare. It includes severe self-injury such as limb amputation, eye removal, and castration—the removal of a male's testicles.

Major self-injury is most often carried out by people who have severe mental health problems or by people who are under the influence of drugs or alcohol.

- Stereotypic self-injuring behavior is repetitive. People with profound intellectual disability or autism, for example, may bang their heads repeatedly to get attention, express frustration, or for other reasons.

- Moderate/superficial self-injury includes cutting, burning, and other types of self-injury, such as those performed by Princess Diana and so many other people today.

The Sociology of Self-Injury

Sociologists study social structures. They study how people behave with each other

BRANDING

Branding is a type of burning self-injury. People have branded themselves throughout history to show membership in a group or as an initiation rite. Today, young people may brand themselves as a form of body modification, such as with fraternity or sorority letters. Some may self-brand to show courage or to bond with others. Others use branding as an emotional release. Branding objects might be a heated coin, bottle cap, key, paper clip, or coat hanger—whatever is at hand.

WHEN IS BODY DECORATION SELF-INJURY?

Wendy Lader, cofounder of a self-injury treatment program, explained to the *Chicago Tribune* that normal, healthy teens use tattoos and piercings to assert their individuality. What separates body modification from self-injury, she says, is motivation. When the desire for a new tattoo or body piercing turns into a need, it then moves into the realm of self-injury.[5]

and within societies. A 2009 study on self-injury found 43.6 percent of the study's subjects said they started self-injuring because they knew someone else who did it or they learned about it through media.[3] Other studies have come to similar conclusions: teens, especially girls, are strongly influenced by friends who self-injure.

Sociologists Peter and Patricia Adler have researched the social reasons for why young people start self-injuring. They believe young people come to see self-injury as an acceptable way to deal with anger, confusion, and frustration. Through friends and the media, they also learn how to self-injure. The Adlers see today's growing trend of self-injury as "a practice of individuals who lack severe trauma in their lives but who turn to this behavior as a means of self-expression, comfort, affiliation, identification, sexuality, and rebellion, for myriad reasons."[4]

The Biology of Self-Injury

To explain why people self-injure, biologists point to the role of brain chemicals that regulate pain and pleasure. A person with a chemical imbalance in the brain, for example, might feel little physical pain. This person might self-injure in order to feel something. There is also a concept in biology called biological reinforcement. The idea is that pain from self-injury produces endorphins— hormones in the brain and nervous system that help to reduce pain. When endorphins are released, a person feels euphoric or "high." Similar to drug use, a person will continue self-injuring to feel that rush of endorphins.

Though each of these sciences looks at self-injury from a different point of view, together they lead to a greater understanding of self-injury. As recent as 50 years ago, practically no theories of self-injury existed. Similar to the spread of the behavior itself, the study of self-injury has also grown.

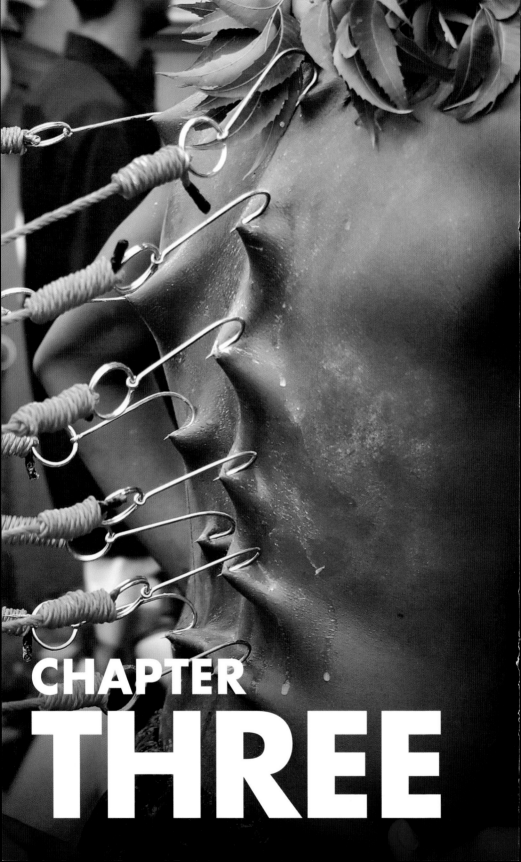

CHAPTER
THREE

THE HISTORY OF SELF-INJURY

Self-injury is nothing new. It has been around for centuries, practiced mostly for religious and spiritual reasons. In the late 1800s, the first psychologists observed patients with mental health problems who injured themselves. But it wasn't until the mid-1900s that scientists began to formally study the behavior. Theories about self-injury are still evolving.

In many cultures, self-injury was a spiritual practice. When people injured themselves, the pain they felt disconnected them from normal life and connected them instead with a god or spirit. In the Sufi branch of Islam, men would insert skewers and spikes into their bodies. They might swallow glass and razor blades, hold red-hot metal to their skin and teeth, and eat poisonous snakes and scorpions. Witnesses claimed the men felt no pain, spilled no blood, and their wounds healed right away. The Sufis considered these feats miracles.

In Singapore, Hindus take part in a procession known as Thaipusam, in which some participants walk with hooks embedded in their backs.

As part of the sun dance ceremony, members of Native-American Plains tribes pierced their bodies with large hooks, which were attached to tall poles. Hoisted into the air, the participants stared at the sun. They hoped to receive spiritual visions that would guide their lives.

Throughout history, many people have self-injured in the name of religion. In Christianity, the crucifixion of Christ is sometimes thought of as self-injury, since Christ willingly accepted his suffering. After Christ's

CULTURAL RITES AND CUSTOMS

Self-injury plays a role in many cultural rites and customs. In some cultures, people injure themselves as a way to help their society. For example, in the Abidji tribe in Ivory Coast, Africa, a man will stab himself with a knife. As the wound heals, it mirrors the healing taking place within his community.

Sometimes self-injury is performed as ritual mourning. In the Pacific Islands, and in some Native-American tribes, people have cut off their fingertips after the deaths of close relatives. In some cultures, self-injury has been used as a status symbol. In ancient China, people admired the small feet of dancers. To copy the dancers' small feet, girls' feet were bound in early childhood to keep them from growing. Though a sign of the upper classes, it had the result of crippling the women, who could barely stand as a result of the binding.

Tattooing has been practiced for thousands of years by many cultures. The Maori of New Zealand have used tattoos to show their individuality and to scare their enemies. In Japan, Geishas tattooed their bodies to enhance their beauty. Tattooed mummies have been found in Egypt, and tattooing is mentioned in the Bible.

death, Christians began whipping themselves to copy his experience and to relieve religious guilt. People have cut out their tongues, blinded themselves, or cut off their genitals as offerings to God. Other people believe God told them to self-injure. In early Christianity, a few self-injurers were even elevated to sainthood. Some self-injuring religious practices continue today. In Western cultures, some people still scar and pierce their bodies for spiritual reasons.

1800s to 1940s

Modern psychology began in the late 1800s. Early psychologists believed people who self-injured were trying to commit suicide. The famous psychologist Sigmund Freud believed both suicide and self-injury were part of the human instinct toward life and death.

CULTURAL REASONS FOR SELF-INJURY

Fakir Musafar, an expert on body-modification, has found 12 different reasons to explain why people in tribal societies pierce, mark, or modify their bodies:
- Rites of passage
- Peer bonding
- Respect for elders and ancestors
- Status symbol or sign of bravery, courage, or belonging
- Initiation
- Protection
- Opening to spirits
- Body or spirit rebalancing
- Physical healing of self or others
- Spiritual healing of self or others
- Community healing or tribal bonding
- Connecting community to greater forces

Sigmund Freud argued self-injury and suicide were one and the same.

Freud's views were so influential that a theory of
self-injury separate from suicide did not appear until
1938. That year, physician Karl Menninger wrote his
book *Man Against Himself.* Menninger claimed acts of
self-injury were actually attempts to avoid suicide by
sacrificing a small part of the body.

1960s and 1970s: "Wrist-Cutting Syndrome"

Thirty years after Menninger's book was published, researchers found more differences between self-injury and suicide. In a 1967 journal article, psychiatric researchers Harold Graff and Richard Mallin described a "wrist-cutting syndrome." In this syndrome, the typical wrist cutter was a young, nice-looking unmarried woman who had problems with sex, became addicted easily, and could not connect with people.

During the 1970s, researchers presented more data on wrist-cutting syndrome. In one study, female self-cutters were found to share similar backgrounds, which included eating disorders and physical trauma.[1] These

DSM-5

When someone goes to a doctor with an illness, they get a diagnosis based on their symptoms. When someone goes to a mental health expert, they also get a diagnosis based on their symptoms. Mental health experts in the United States turn to a book called the *Diagnostic and Statistical Manual of Mental Disorders* (DSM) to help them diagnose a patient's illness. Until recently, self-injury was only mentioned in the *DSM* as a symptom of other mental illnesses. But in May 2013, NSSI was added to the newest edition of the manual, the *DSM-5*. Though it is listed as a condition needing further research, proponents are encouraged. They hope the addition of NSSI to the manual will bring more awareness to the behavior and kick-start more research.

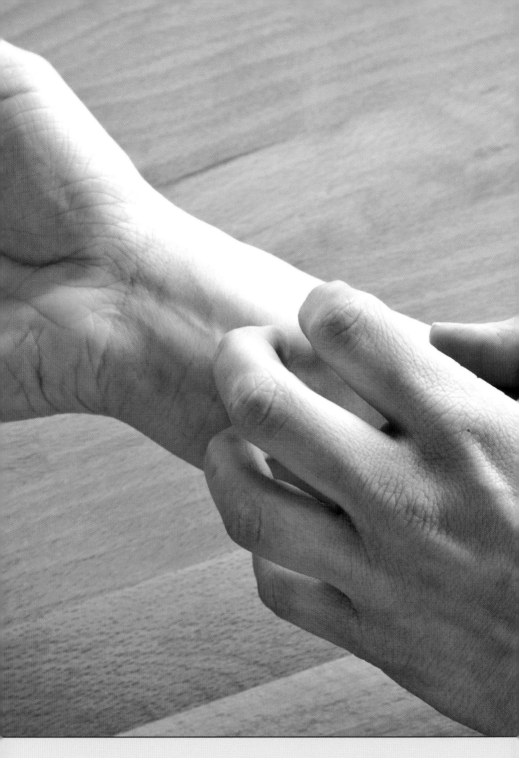

Research data in the 1970s showed self-injury included
scratching and gouging in addition to cutting.

women also felt empty emotionally. One of the study researchers thought "wrist-cutting syndrome" was no longer a good term for the behavior, because subjects were also cutting other parts of their bodies. And they weren't just cutting. They were also scratching and gouging themselves, and even rubbing their bodies with bits of glass.

1980s: Changing Theories and Growing Interest

Researchers were finally coming to the conclusion suicide was not the goal of most people who injured themselves. In a 1979 journal article, English researcher Richard J. Turner renamed parasuicidal behavior "non-fatal deliberate self-harm." Then psychiatric researchers J. Kahan and E. M. Pattison began what would become the modern interest in self-injury. In 1983, they came up with an idea they called "deliberate self-harm syndrome." Kahan and Pattison began categorizing the self-harm incidents of their research subjects by the number of episodes, types of self-harm, duration of the behavior, and reason for self-harming. They believed people self-harmed because they could not control their impulses.

While researching self-injury for a conference presentation during the 1980s, Dr. Favazza found material on a bloodletting ceremony in Morocco that was meant to heal a person's illness. Fascinated, Favazza wondered if self-injury in Western cultures might also serve some kind of healing purpose. Favazza's research led him to write *Bodies Under Siege: Self-Mutilation in Culture and Psychiatry*, an exploration of self-injury across cultures published in 1987. It was the first major book on the subject since Karl Menninger's *Man Against Himself* in 1938.

1990s: A Hot Topic

It wasn't until the mid-1990s that mental health professionals and the public paid much attention to self-injury. Similar to eating disorders, self-mutilation brought up fears of a dark activity people wanted to ignore. People who cut and burned themselves often showed up in therapists' offices and were thought to be very mentally ill.

With Favazza's book came more interest in self-injury from mental health professionals. Not only was it now a growing topic of research, but the shocking admissions of cutting by Princess Diana and Johnny Depp also made it a hot topic in the media and with the public. Self-injury lost some of its stigma, and—for better or worse—celebrities and noncelebrities alike were sharing their self-injury experiences with each other and with the world. Self-injury seemed to be a growing way to manage emotional pain.

CHAPTER
FOUR

WHO SELF-INJURES AND WHY

The stereotypical cutter is a teenage girl who was abused as a child, has other problems at home, uses drugs, is failing in school, and has friends who also self-injure. In many cases, this is true. The people at greatest risk for self-injuring are:

- Females

- Teens or young adults

- Teens with friends who also self-injure

- Teens overwhelmed with life issues

- Teens dealing with mental health issues

- Teens using alcohol and drugs

But as with all stereotypes, this one is not always true. For example, studies have shown at least 30 percent of teens who self-injure are boys.[1] Experts

Contrary to gender stereotypes, males also self-injure, and some experts believe many male cases go unreported.

point out that boys may show up in self-injury statistics less than girls because they tend to act out by hitting themselves, banging their heads, or punching things. These injuries leave wounds that can easily be explained as a result of fights, accidents, or contact sports.

Sexual abuse is a risk factor in some cases, but many young people who harm themselves come from stable two-parent homes where there is no abuse. And it is not just teens who self-injure. The practice can continue well into adulthood—and even begin in adulthood.

Other Risk Factors

Even with these exceptions, there are factors that can make someone more susceptible to self-injury. Some self-injurers have mental health issues, such as depression or anxiety, which add to a sense of despair. Young

Bullying can take the form of emotional, verbal, and physical abuse, which can all lead to self-injury.

people who have gone through some kind of trauma, such as witnessing a disaster, or physical, emotional, or sexual abuse, can also be at greater risk of self-injuring. Emotional abuse is a very common risk factor for self-injury when young people are taught not to value their emotions. While abuse usually happens at home, it might come from outside the family, such as from a bully or a caretaker.

Research shows a stressful birth or being hospitalized as an infant can lower mood-regulating hormones, which can later lead to self-injury. It also seems a tendency to self-injure may be inherited from one's family. Self-injury happens among all racial groups, but it is more common among the poor and those who lack social support. It also seems gay, lesbian, bisexual, and transgendered youth are at greater risk for self-injury. So why are people injuring themselves?

Controlling Emotional Distress

People often self-injure for two reasons that may seem opposite from each other: to numb their pain or to keep from feeling numb. Jane, a cheerleader in high school who came from a well-adjusted family, burned herself with a heated coin when the stress in her life became too overwhelming: "It was just this intense emotion of anxiety and panic and pressure and frustration, and all of a sudden it was a release," she told an interviewer.[3] For people like Jane, self-injury serves as a valve that shuts down strong feelings. It gives them a sense of control.

Judy, a college student majoring in music therapy, explained to a researcher why she cut herself: "I wanted to be able to feel because I swung from depression to complete numbness. It's better to feel pain than nothing."[7] For people like Judy, whose feelings are shut down, cutting makes them feel again. They use the pain as a way to jump-start their emotions.

SELF-INJURY AND DEVELOPMENTAL DISABILITIES

Some disabled children use self-injury as a form of communication. Children with developmental delays or autism often have trouble speaking. They become frustrated when they cannot find words to express themselves. These children may bang their heads, poke their eyes, or scratch or bite themselves to express their frustration. The behavior helps these children get attention and help from caregivers.

What Judy and Jane have in common is their inability to cope with emotional distress in a healthy way. They also want to gain some control over their emotions. Emotional stress can come from many sources. People who self-injure often report they have problems with relationships, they don't know where they fit in the world, and they are sexually confused. They also report feeling intense pressure and strong feelings, such as anger, sadness, despair, hurt, frustration, shame, guilt, isolation, and rejection. These are not the only reasons people choose to self-injure.

Self-Punishment

Similarly to Princess Diana, who said she hurt herself because she wanted help, some people self-injure because they believe they have no other way to express their pain. The physical injury—be it a cut, burn, or

BORDERLINE PERSONALITY DISORDER

Self-injury is one of the symptoms of the mental health disorder borderline personality disorder (BPD). Some mental health experts believe Princess Diana may have suffered with BPD. People with BPD tend to have unstable relationships and stormy emotions. They have wide mood swings and fear abandonment. They also tend to be impulsive and angry. In addition to self-injuring, people with BPD can be suicidal and struggle with depression and substance abuse. The disorder occurs equally in men and women.

It has long been thought BPD was a result of childhood trauma, such as from abuse or neglect. But new studies are showing people may inherit a likelihood to get the disorder. Symptoms of BPD can start at a very young age, even if a child has a normal upbringing. Children who are later diagnosed with BPD have been shown to be moodier, more anxious, and more sensitive than other children. They also tend to have fewer friends. Experts believe people with BPD misinterpret other people's feelings and actions. They may even misinterpret facial expressions. There are quite a few people with BPD. A US government study published in 2008 put the figure at 6 percent of the general public.[8] That is double past estimates. This knowledge helps mental health experts make the right diagnosis when working with patients who self-injure.

bruise—shows the outside world what the self-injurer is feeling inside. Self-injurers believe no one is listening; they wish someone would.

Others self-injure as a form of self-punishment. While interviewing self-injurers, one researcher spoke to a young woman who believed she needed to punish herself for being so awful. Another young woman felt that if she didn't punish herself, no one was going to do it for her. Mental health experts have found overly aggressive discipline from a parent can cause children to later direct anger toward themselves. It has also been found that some children who are victims of emotional or physical abuse learn to connect pain with love—the abuse may have been negative, but it was at least some kind of attention.

Fitting In and Rebelling

Young people may try self-injuring just to fit in simply because everyone else is doing it. Similarly, if a group of friends is self-injuring, a member of the group may feel pressured to join in, even if it is not something he or she would otherwise do. As a result of teens self-injuring in order to fit in, the behavior can spread quickly when it gains attention at school and online.

Cutting was accepted as part of the goth culture in the 1980s and 1990s.

Over the past few decades, groups who reject mainstream society have used cutting and other forms of self-injury. In the 1970s and 1980s, punk-rockers were into drug use, body piercing, and cutting themselves with razor blades. In the early 1980s, goths (short for "gothic") branched off from hardcore punks. Goths dressed in black, and blood and violence were part of the goth music scene. When the dark-and-brooding subculture moved into high schools, cutting went along with it. By the 2000s, goths had been replaced by emos (short for "emotional"). In high schools, emo kids were labeled as emotional, sensitive, introverted, and full of anxiety. Self-injury was also a part of this subculture's lifestyle. One former emo noted to an interviewer, "[Cutting] almost became kind of the style, and you accepted the style, and everyone knew who we were and kind of knew [that we self-injured] but turned a blind eye to what we did."[9]

People who self-injure come from many backgrounds and use the behavior for different reasons. But the results of self-injury are not quite so varied. Simply put, self-injury is addictive and it is dangerous.

SELF-INJURY AMONG PRISON INMATES

Self-injury is common in prisons, and cutting among inmates can even become contagious. Like the general population, inmates use cutting and other forms of self-injury as a way to cope with emotional pain. They also use it as a form of rebellion, to manipulate prison staff (for example, to get moved to a different unit), or to get medical help.

CHAPTER FIVE

CONSEQUENCES OF SELF-INJURY

Most people who self-injure do not intend to commit suicide. And most people who self-injure stop the behavior without treatment. But self-injury can have serious short-term and long-term emotional and physical consequences.

The relief from self-injury is only temporary. The behavior does not solve the underlying problems the self-injurer is facing, which means the problems are still there after the calming effects of the self-injury have worn off. Then the self-injurer is left feeling intense shame and guilt about his or her behavior. The hiding, stress, and lying associated with self-injury take a toll, leading to further isolation, lowered self-esteem, and the need to self-injure to deal with these negative feelings. Sometimes the problems and emotional pain can lead to a suicide attempt.

While isolation and depression may be factors leading one to self-injure, they are also consequences of the behavior.

Self-injury can be addictive. A teen who used to cut herself told *Girls' Life* magazine, "Once I started cutting, I needed it more and more to maintain control. I got to the point where I liked cutting and I'd cut just because I wanted to, not because something was upsetting me."[1] Especially at risk for physical problems are self-injurers for whom the behavior has become an addiction. "Like a drug, people tell us that they end up needing more and more to be able to feel OK," Wendy Lader, president of the treatment program S.A.F.E. (Self Abuse Finally Ends) Alternatives, told *Current Health*.[2] A cutter may start cutting on a part of the body that produces more blood loss. He or she may cut deeper. Deep cuts may need stitches or even result in life-threatening blood loss. Infections can set in from wounds or from the use of dirty cutting objects. If enough blood is lost or if infections are not treated, a cut can even result in death.

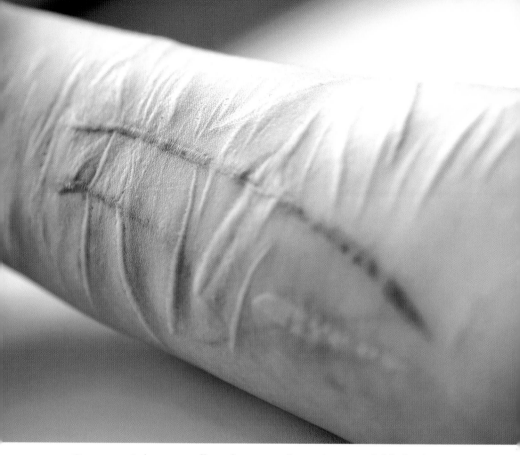

One cosmetic long-term effect of cutting is the evident scars left behind.

Long-Term Risks

While the relief from self-injury is temporary, the dangers are not. Cutters may believe their scars can be surgically removed, but there is very little that can be done—the marks are essentially permanent. Besides blood loss from deep cuts, cutting can result in injured tendons, nerves, and muscles. While some of these injuries can be repaired, cutting a major nerve in the wrist can result in permanent numbness or weakness in the hand. Using acids or chemicals to burn the skin can cause loss of limbs and be life threatening. Repeated head banging can result in permanent brain damage. Self-poisoning and drug overdoses can seriously damage the liver and kidneys.

For people with mental health disorders, self-injury can make these conditions worse. For example, the shame, guilt, and lowered self-esteem linked to self-injury can increase depression and anxiety. Substance abuse can also rise, which increases the risk of self-injuring while under the influence of alcohol or drugs. Drugs and alcohol can impair judgment and make people more impulsive. The combination of impaired judgment and impulsivity can lead to dangerous self-injuries, such as deeper and more dangerous cuts, and even suicide.

Risk of Suicide

Research shows people who injure themselves are not generally trying to commit suicide. One study found 60 percent of those

> "I self-harmed for five years, usually cutting around once a week. Eventually, I'd cut so much that I was starting to lose feeling in my left wrist and, over a period of a few months, I completely lost feeling from my elbow down to my hand."[4]
>
> —Lara

who self-injure have never had suicidal thoughts. And self-injury is approximately 40 to 100 times more common than completed suicide in childhood or adolescence.[5] Some people who self-injure say the emotional release they get from self-injuring actually keeps them from acting on their suicidal thoughts.

But compared to people who do not self-injure, those who do self-injure have a greater risk of suicide. For example, the underlying problems leading someone to self-injure can lead to committing suicide. Also, injuring the body while feeling overly emotional can make suicide more likely. People who self-injure and those who are suicidal have a few things in common. Both have higher than normal levels of anxiety, depression, self-blame, problems with parents, and low self-esteem. They are also more likely to have friends

NEED FOR SENSITIVITY

Medical staff in emergency rooms and urgent-care clinics are not always sensitive to the needs of patients who self-injure. There have been instances of self-injuring patients being denied anesthesia for stitches and treated rudely. The mistreatment can lead self-injurers who already feel unworthy to feel even more so. As a result, they may be less likely to seek medical help in the future and risk infections and other complications. Medical staff is encouraged to treat people with self-injuries as they would treat people with any other type of wound.

who self-injure or have suicidal thoughts, and they believe they have few people they can confide in.

Even though most self-inflicted cuts are intentionally superficial and the bleeding is not life-threatening, experts still warn that self-injury should be taken seriously. It is a sign someone is not coping with overwhelming feelings in a healthy way.

Effect on Others

Self-injurers tend to hide their self-injuring activity from others. Studies show they also tend to hide all of their thoughts and feelings from others. The burden of guilt and secrecy self-injurers feel can affect everything in their life, from what they wear, to relationships, and to the kinds of sports in which they participate.

Thinking people will react to their behavior with shock or disgust, self-injurers shy away from relationships. One study of a group of people who self-injured showed that almost 84 percent hid their self-injury from family members and 66 percent hid their behavior from friends.[6] Subjects in the study said they did not want to burden or frighten loved ones or make them feel guilty or responsible. They also believed their families would not understand their behavior, and the self-injurers wanted to avoid their relatives' negative reactions. Friends of self-injurers often said they did not tell on their self-injuring friend because they feared their friends' rejection.

When family and friends learn a loved one is self-injuring, they may feel a range of emotions. Some may feel anger. They might have trouble understanding why the loved one is injuring him or herself and why the self-injurer cannot stop. Other family and friends may feel guilty, blaming themselves for the self-injurer's

SELF-INJURY, FEAR, AND SECRECY

Most people who self-injure keep their behavior a secret from family and friends. A mental health organization in Britain asked young people who self-injured why this was the case. The most common answer given was fear.[7] Self-injuring was how these young people coped with their problems and they believed it was the only thing keeping them going. They feared if they told someone, their coping strategy would be taken away. These young people also kept their behavior a secret because they feared they would not be taken seriously. Girls especially worried they would be called stupid or people would think they were just looking for attention. Boys often kept their self-injury a secret because they did not think it was important. They tried not to think about it and convinced themselves they would not do it again.

These young people also feared that if anyone found out they self-injured, it would affect their futures. They worried careers such as teaching, nursing, and child care would be off-limits because self-injurers were considered "dangerous." They feared that if they told even one person they self-injured, there would be no way to stop that person from telling someone else and their self-injury would become public knowledge.

Self-injurers often attempt to keep their behavior a secret from friends and family to avoid shame, guilt, or rejection.

behavior and for not being able to prevent it. Or, friends and relatives may feel ashamed that someone they know and love is choosing to cope with problems in such a drastic way. They may act as if it is no big deal or completely ignore the behavior. Whatever feelings people have when a loved one is self-injuring, everyone in the self-injurer's life is affected. And as more and more people self-injure, more and more people will be touched by it.

"It hurts my family and friends to know that I [cut myself]. They feel I shouldn't have to resort to it and would rather have me talk to them about how I'm feeling. But that doesn't always help. Sometimes I just can't talk—I don't have the words."[8]

—Jessica

CHAPTER
SIX

SELF-INJURY AND SOCIETY

Self-injury is clearly a problem for many young people. The rate of self-injury is high in many developed countries and seems to be increasing. Does this mean there is a self-injury epidemic? Experts disagree. They also disagree on what many people consider the number one reason why self-injury is becoming a more acceptable behavior: celebrities and the media.

Self-injury spans the globe. In Australia, the rate of self-injury in teens ages 15 to 19 was found in one study to be 17 percent for girls and 12 percent for boys.[1] In the United Kingdom, a study put the rate of self-injury at approximately 20 percent for teen girls and 7 percent for teen boys.[2] In Denmark, a 2011 study found 16.2 percent of teens said they had injured themselves during the previous 12 months. In two other studies from 2011, 15 percent of Chinese teens

The number of teens self-injuring continues to rise, leading some experts to believe media's increasing focus on it is to blame.

INTERNATIONAL CONTAGION

Unlike the middle of the last century, when news was limited primarily to local newspapers and national radio and television programs, media outlets and the Internet now span the globe. News is released instantaneously. A celebrity revelation, song, or movie about cutting can be accessed practically anywhere at any time. And because problems with coping and emotional turmoil are common to adolescents everywhere, self-injury has become an international problem.

and 13.71 percent of Belgian teens claimed they had injured themselves over their lifetimes.[3]

Many studies prove rates of self-injury are rising. In 2013, the number of young people treated in UK hospitals for self-injury rose 11 percent compared with 2012. Hospital treatment for self-injury involving UK children ages 10 to 14 jumped 30 percent.[4] In 2013, ChildLine, a UK children's charity, saw a 167 percent increase in young people contacting them for help with self-injuring.[5] For many experts, these numbers speak for themselves: self-injury is on the rise.

Yet at least one study has found the rates of self-injury leveled off between 2005 and 2011.[6] And some experts believe reports of self-injury are overblown. They say the behavior has always been here; people are simply noticing and reporting it more. Whether or not self-injury is on the rise, it does exist and young people and their families and friends are suffering because of it. Of the various healthy and unhealthy ways teens might choose to deal with their stress, why do so many choose to self-injure? A number of people point to celebrities and the media as the primary culprits.

Celebrity Influence

In the 1990s, after Princess Diana and other celebrities began admitting they self-injured, self-injury began

EATING DISORDERS AND SELF-INJURY

When celebrities reveal they self-injure, they often disclose another injurious behavior: an eating disorder. Eating disorders include anorexia nervosa and bulimia. A study published in 2010 by the *Journal of Adolescent Health* showed there is a link between self-injury and eating disorders. Among 630 patients with eating disorders who were screened for self-injury, 41 percent admitted to cutting or burning themselves.[7] Mental health experts believe the two behaviors are connected by anxiety disorders. People with eating disorders

experience extreme anxiety, which cutting helps to relieve. Richard Pesikoff, professor of psychiatry at Baylor College of Medicine, told ABC News, "People [with eating disorders] do a variety of self-soothing behaviors like rocking, picking, or cutting. The eating soothes the anxiety, but creates a new set of problems. Then they worry about being fat. Then [they] have to resolve that. Then they cut."[8] Some people with eating disorders have also been found to self-injure in order to punish themselves.

Actress Christina Ricci has admitted to and condoned the practice of self-injury.

popping up in movies, newspaper stories, television programs, and song lyrics. Some experts believe self-injury would not be so widespread without musicians, actors, and other celebrities admitting to its use. They say that because a famous person self-injures, vulnerable teens then see the behavior as an acceptable way to handle emotional pain.

Some celebrities do not go out of their way to discourage the practice. For example, actress Christina Ricci admitted to a *SPIN* magazine reporter that she put out cigarettes on her arms: "You get this endorphin rush," she explained. "It takes a second, a little sting, and then it's like you don't feel anything. It's calming, actually."[9] Rocker Marilyn Manson has cut himself on stage and shows off his cutting scars.

But not everyone agrees the media has much of an impact on self-injury or that celebrity revelations are even a bad thing. Some argue that

OTHER CELEBRITIES WHO SELF-INJURE

In a 1998 interview with *Rolling Stone* magazine, singer Fiona Apple revealed she suffered with depression, low self-esteem, and an eating disorder. She began scratching after her first bad music review. Sometimes she would bite her lip until it bled: "I have a little bit of a problem with that," she explained in the interview. "It's a common thing. . . . I know, it's bad. But it's not like a hobby of mine. It just makes you *feel.*"[10]

Megan Fox, star of the *Transformers* movies, has acknowledged she cut herself to manage her feelings of insecurity and lack of self-worth. But, she told *Rolling Stone* magazine in 2009, "I would never call myself a cutter. Girls go through different phases when they're growing up, when they're miserable and do different things, whether it's an eating disorder or they dabble in cutting."[11]

Singer Demi Lovato now shares her stories of self-injury in
hopes of helping other self-injurers feel less isolated.

people who attempt self-injury after watching a film
or hearing a celebrity speak about it are most likely
already predisposed to the behavior and would have
self-injured anyway. Some believe celebrity revelations
of self-injury can actually be a good thing. They say it
brings needed attention to a secretive practice that might
otherwise go unnoticed. Reading about a famous person
who cuts her arms, for example, may make an isolated
young person who also cuts feel less alone. When Demi
Lovato, singer and former Disney star, talked about her
problems with cutting and bulimia on an MTV special

in October 2010, she explained why she made her self-injury public: "I know that some girl probably needed to hear this story tonight."[12] Celebrities can also serve as role models when they stop the practice. Angelina Jolie, who has mentioned in several interviews that she cut herself when she was a teen, admits it is a dangerous practice and something she no longer does.[13]

Whether self-injury represents an epidemic of copycat behavior or increased awareness about an already-existing behavior, the rise in hospitalizations does suggest self-injury has at least taken a more serious turn. In addition to the media, many experts blame the Internet as another reason for the rise in self-injury.

SONG LYRICS ABOUT SELF-INJURY

Self-injury has been a part of the punk rock, goth, and emo music movements for years, and the subject commonly appears in song lyrics. The following are a few examples:

- "Then she closed her eyes/And found relief in a knife/The blood flows as she cries." From "The Way She Feels" by Between the Trees
- "I have been here many times before/Hurt myself again today/And, the worst part is there's no one else to blame." From "Breathe Me" by Sia
- "I hurt myself today/To see if I still feel/I focus on the pain/the only thing that's real." From "Hurt" by Nine Inch Nails/Johnny Cash
- "Sweet and divine/Razor of mine/Sweet and divine/Razorblade shine." From "Razor" by Foo Fighters

CHAPTER
SEVEN

SELF-INJURY AND THE INTERNET

Images of self-inflicted wounds abound on the Internet. Video "how-tos" showing cutting techniques are easily accessible. There are blogs and websites promoting self-injury as a lifestyle. Cutters share tips, advice, poetry, and stories on message boards. Clearly, there is a proliferation of self-injury on the Internet. As with celebrity revelations, does it serve a purpose by providing a resource for lonely and isolated teens? Or does if reflect a serious health crisis?

John Powell, a researcher at the University of Oxford, England, told the *Washington Post* in 2013, "I think this whole area of '[self-]harm blogs' is the most contentious area, with both academics and clinicians, as regards to whether the Internet is more of a force for good or harm in health care. There is no consensus on where the balance lies."[1]

Some self-injurers find comfort on the Internet through online communication with other self-injurers.

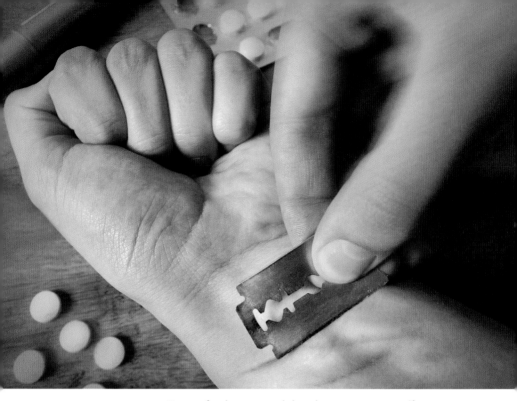

Critics of online accessibility claim some teens self-injure just so they can post photos of it on the Internet.

Some people see the Internet as a force for good. Teens who struggle with fitting in at school and at home say they find thousands of like-minded friends on the Web. "It's just that everyone feels the same," said a young woman about blogging on the popular site Tumblr. "I know they're not going to judge me for self-harming. It's nice to know that you can tell your story without being judged."[2]

But experts say there are drawbacks to all of this easy access to explicit self-injury information:

- When online bonds are formed with other self-injurers, the habit can become harder to break; self-injuring may seem normal and even healthy.

- Self-injury can become competitive. Cutters have been known to see if they can use the same cutting technique they see someone else using online. Members of Internet pro-self-injury groups, or "cutting clubs," urge each other to be more extreme in their self-injury.

- Some blogs spread disinformation about how to self-injure or about treatments that do not work.

- A teen's judgment is not as fully formed as an adult's, which means teens are more easily convinced that what they see online is true.

- Seeing online images of wounds or people self-injuring can trigger a relapse in someone who is trying to stop the behavior.

- Self-injury websites may make self-injurers feel less alone. But without information on how to change, the person can be left with a sense of hopelessness.

- Given the web's free and open nature, keeping self-injury off the Internet is unlikely. But some sites are trying to clamp down on the worst offenders.

Cutting Blogs

In February 2012, pressured mostly by eating disorder advocacy groups, the Internet blogging host site Tumblr

TEENS ARE "WIRED" TO TAKE RISKS

Teens are more likely to take part in self-injury and other risks than adults. One reason for this may be how the brain changes as people age. In children, the brain's systems that process emotions (the amygdala) and higher thinking (the cortex) are both immature. In early adolescence, emotional processing grows quickly but higher thinking does not mature until people reach their mid-20s. That means teens can be overwhelmed with emotions but do not have the skills to deal with them. This leads to stress. And because emotion and thinking are not balanced, teens often choose risky behavior— such as self-injury—to reduce their stress.

Many studies have shown risky behavior is a side effect of being a teen. One study found 75 percent of deaths among 10- to 24-year-olds were from preventable causes, such as car accidents and suicide.[3] Another study measured the reactions of 86 men and boys while they played computer games. The teens in the study group made risky choices more often, and 14-year-olds showed the riskiest behavior.[4] Studies have also shown the likelihood of teens taking risks increases when they are with friends. The immature brain provides one explanation as to why teens choose self-injuring behavior to begin with and why it increases when teens are among friends.

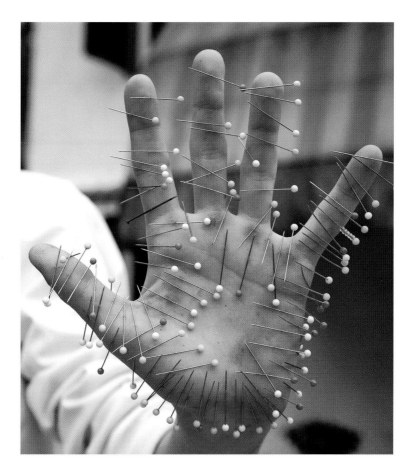

While cutting blogs and websites are most common, blogs and online videos also center on other forms of self-injury, such as piercing.

banned blogs on its service that "glorified" eating disorders and self-injury. The site also said it would start showing public service announcements for anyone searching keywords such as "self-harm." But a year and a half later, self-injury blogs were still easily found on Tumblr. SimilarWeb, a firm that tracks and analyzes web data, estimated 197,200 blogs on Tumblr used language related to self-injury and eating disorders.[5] In France, researchers have theorized that Internet bans send self-injurers underground, where it is more difficult for advocacy groups to find them.

Self-Injury Videos

In 2011, researchers noted that self-injury, especially cutting, made up 14 to 24 percent of the top videos on YouTube. The 100 top self-injuring videos received more than 2 million page views.[6] Like Tumblr, YouTube has tried to reduce the number of self-injury videos by flagging and removing videos that are too graphic. Self-injury advocacy groups worried the videos were making self-injury seem mainstream and causing viewers to imitate the behavior they saw. David Prior, executive director of a self-injury treatment program in Utah, told *Girls' Life* magazine, "Unfortunately, girls are teaching each other how to cut. Having visual examples of cutting increases the likelihood of them doing it because young women see how accessible and easy it can be."[8]

But other experts do not believe it is clear videos cause people who watch them to start self-injuring. Dr. Keith Ablow, a psychiatrist who treats self-injurers, wrote in a Fox News article, "I don't think the videos are likely to spark any epidemic of self-injury. If anything, I think the videos are more likely to encourage the many, many people who believe their self-mutilating behavior is too shameful to admit to finally talk about it and to, hopefully, get help."[9] Other experts suggest that parents who discover their children looking at self-injury videos can use the opportunity to discuss the topic with them.

Help in Quitting

While looking at pro-self-injury sites can make recovery harder, taking part in pro-recovery websites can help recovery. For people trying to quit,

"Cutting pushed me away from people. I locked myself in my room and watched cutting videos. I thought I was connecting with people by watching them. But I really wasn't connecting with anyone."[10]
—A girl who self-injured and is now in recovery

BULLYING AND SELF-INJURY

Today the Internet is making the bullying-self-injury connection even more complicated. Bullying is a major stressor capable of leading teens to start self-injuring. In one study, 66 percent of teens who self-injured said they had been bullied.[12] To make matters worse, researchers have found teens are most at risk for the depression and anxiety that lead to self-injury at the same time they are most likely to be victims of bullying. "In my day, if someone was bullied, they could find escape at home, but that isn't available now," British clinical specialist Sue Minto told an interviewer. "Before you know it, something you said in confidence . . . is up there in neon lights for anyone to read for any amount of time."[13]

groups and chat rooms with like-minded members can be a good distraction when someone is fighting the urge to self-injure. Members support and encourage one another and share success stories. They also serve as cheerleaders when a self-injurer relapses; members have been through the same thing and can help other self-injurers feel less isolated and alone. "When you find a safe board where there's not that many triggers it can actually be a really positive thing," a woman in recovery told an interviewer. "It can be a supportive environment that actually helps you to stop or supports you when you're trying to stop."[11]

Whether self-injury on the Internet is positive or negative seems to depend on one's point of view. It also seems to depend upon the stage at which the self-injurer is—wanting support in their addiction or support in their recovery. Both sides are easily found online.

TRIGGERS

One of the biggest complaints about the rise of videos and other online sites dedicated to self-injury is that they can be highly triggering. A trigger is any kind of sensory cue—sound, sight, taste, touch, or scent—that brings up feelings and memories having to do with an addiction. For example, seeing an online photo of a cut wrist or listening to or reading about a person's recent burning experience can create an urge to cut or burn. This is especially serious for people trying to recover. Even if an addicted self-injurer has kept away from the behavior for several months, a strong trigger can send that person right back to the behavior as if no time has passed.

CHAPTER
EIGHT

WHAT'S BEING DONE ABOUT SELF-INJURY?

Whether or not self-injury is an epidemic, and whether or not the media and Internet are helping to fuel it, young people are injuring themselves. And it is generally agreed they are doing so more seriously and in greater numbers than ever before. Unless teens' self-injuring sends them to an emergency room or they wind up in a counselor's office because they have a mental health disorder, young people do not often seek help. They fear they will be misunderstood, not taken seriously, or thought to be mentally ill. That means it is often up to a parent, teacher, or someone else in the self-injurer's life to notice the problem. But not many parents and teachers are aware of self-injury or know what to do about it.

Because most self-injurers do not seek assistance, it is important for close friends and family to step in and help.

The following are warning signs of self-injuring:

- Wearing long sleeves and long pants all of the time, even in hot weather

- Not taking part in activities that show skin, such as swimming

- Scars from cuts, burns, etc.

- Fresh cuts, burns, or other wounds

- Bruises

- Broken bones

- Frequent claims of accidents or mishaps

- Excuses for injuries that do not make sense

- Hidden supply of blades and bandages

- Keeping sharp objects on hand

- Low self-esteem

- Spending lots of time alone

- Sudden mood shifts

- Difficulty getting along with other people

Abusing drugs and alcohol may be a sign your
friend is unhappy and is also self-injuring.

- Depression, statements of helplessness
  and hopelessness

- Eating disorders

- Substance abuse

Self-Injury Policies

Some countries, such as Britain, have national guidelines for dealing with and managing self-injury. There are no national self-injury policies in the United States. Government-based attempts to reduce the behavior are taking place mostly in school districts. It is not hard to understand why, given how many students self-injure in the United States. A 2007 national survey found 81 percent of school counselors had worked with a teen who had self-injured.[1] School counselors, teachers, and other school staff are often on the front lines of the self-injury problem. Even so, few US schools have formal policies for dealing with self-injury. Education and mental health experts are trying to fill the void by suggesting ways schools can help students who self-injure:

- Schools should teach all school staff about self-injury, instructing them to treat self-injuring students with respect and support.

- School staff should "trust their gut" and not ignore when they think a student is self-injuring.

- Students who self-injure have often experienced trauma and abuse, so it is very important to create a safe environment. These students need structure, consistency, and predictability in their relationships.

- Teens who self-injure report high levels of loneliness, poor social networks, and poor relationships with parents. They also tend to feel invisible. To help students who self-injure feel more connected, teachers should include them in activities that allow the students to feel meaningful and linked to something bigger than themselves.

- Friends show loyalty to their friends more than to adults. It is important to encourage peers to

Mental health experts suggest including self-injurers in daily routines and activities may help them feel less secluded and more confident.

recognize emotional pain and share knowledge about a friend's self-injuring behavior with adults who can help.

At least one school district is taking a high-tech approach to reducing self-injury. The Glendale School District in Southern California has hired a company to collect Internet data on students at its middle schools and high schools. The company, Geo Listening, tracks sites such as Facebook, Twitter, and Instagram. When the company finds posts related to self-injury—in addition to bullying, suicide, threats, and other issues affecting student safety—the company informs the school district. Glendale schools Superintendent Dick Sheehan told the *Los Angeles Times* the system is working well.[2] Even though the company does not hack

TWO EDUCATORS' ADVICE TO OTHER EDUCATORS

Laura A. Dorko Mueller and Matthew D. Selekman, both educators, offer their advice to other educators:

"First, give yourself a break. Remember that even mental health professionals struggle with a feeling of repulsion when presented with this behavior. Take a minute to let yourself feel upset and even disgusted. Once you have had a chance to feel your original reaction, remind yourself of the complicated nature of self-injury. The student has often suffered from various difficulties in their life histories. Self-injury has become an effective coping mechanism for him or her and you need to approach them sympathetically and with a listening ear."[3]— *Laura A. Dorko Mueller*

Selekman offered his advice in the journal *Educational Leadership:*

"At all costs, school personnel need to avoid responding to self-harming students with disgust, anxiety, or fear. They must not lecture the students about the dangers of this behavior, play detective and ask to see their cuts or burn marks, or interrogate and further invalidate them. Instead, they should strive to understand the meaning of this behavior for the student, how the behavior has been helpful and how they can now be helpful to the student. . . . Self-harming students need to know that teachers and other school personnel care about them."[4]

into students' private online accounts, critics say the results of the data gathering could infringe on students' free-speech rights. They also worry students might be disciplined for comments made outside of school.

Raising Awareness

In addition to schools and some governments, private and nonprofit organizations in the United States and abroad are trying to curb self-injury through awareness-raising activities. Self-Injury Awareness Day (SIAD) is a global event held every March 1 to raise awareness of self-injury. Organizers hope the event will lead to greater empathy toward self-injurers, less judgment and fear, and fewer people who suffer in silence. SIAD supporters wear orange and purple wristbands or ribbons. They hand out fact sheets about self-injury to parents, health-care professionals, teachers, friends of self-injurers, and self-injurers themselves. Supporters are encouraged to hold SIAD events

PROJECT TOE

The same social media that may be adding to the increase in self-injury is also trying to help those wanting to stop. Project Toe is a smartphone application that helps self-injurers get help from volunteers when they feel the urge to self-injure. Volunteers can also sign up to be helpers at http://www.projecttoe.com.

and e-mail and write letters to politicians, local media, and churches about SIAD, including facts about self-injury.

In the United States, the Self Injury Foundation provides funding for research in addition to advocacy and support for self-injurers, their families, and educators. The goal of the nonprofit organization Adolescent Self Injury Foundation is to raise awareness about adolescent self-injury. It also offers help in the recovery process for young adults who self-injure.

Prevention of self-injury is difficult. While some things are being done to deal with the behavior, there are still gaping holes. For example, as of 2013 there were no organized efforts from celebrities against the practice. Also missing was a solely US-based awareness campaign, such as the international Self-Injury Awareness Day. But that does not mean support does not exist. When a person who self-injures is ready to end his or her behavior, treatment is available.

SOME GOOD NEWS

When it comes to self-injury outcomes, the good news is most teens stop self-injuring in early adulthood. One study found 90 percent of those who self-injured stopped on their own, with 10 percent continuing into adulthood. By age 29, only 1 percent of the study's participants were still self-injuring.[5]

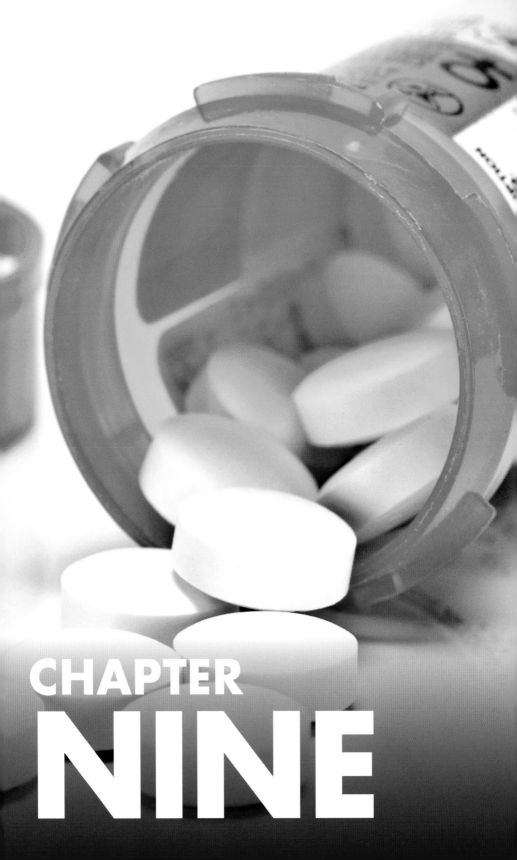

CHAPTER
NINE

TREATMENT: HELPING THOSE WHO SELF-INJURE

O nce a person who self-injures has become addicted to the behavior, stopping can be tough. As with any addiction, recovery can take time, hard work, and a desire to change. There are no medications that directly treat self-injury. But doctors can prescribe drugs to treat underlying mental health problems, such as depression and anxiety.

Most young people who self-injure do not like admitting to their behavior. But doctors and self-injurers in recovery agree one of the most important steps self-injurers can take is to honestly talk about their problems with someone they trust. This might be a relative, teacher, counselor, or friend. In return, one of the most important things doctors, family members, and friends can do is accept and love self-injurers as they are

Medications can help people with conditions such as depression and anxiety feel less compelled to hurt themselves.

and not judge or criticize them. Mental health experts have found that when teens do not feel judged, they are more willing to learn new coping skills.

Providing Help

Experts say the sooner self-injury is detected and treated, the more likely the behavior will end without leaving lasting physical and emotional scars. If you see a friend who you think is self-injuring, stay calm and act normal. You can ask the friend who self-injures if he or she wants help, and if the friend agrees, you can assist in arranging for the friend to see a counselor or other trusted adult.

The self-injurer likely feels ashamed of his or her behavior. Assuming why a person self-injures can cause even more

It is best for friends to be supportive and available to the self-injurer.

distress, which can trigger more self-injuring. That is why it is important for anyone wanting to help a person who self-injures to be as informed as possible about self-injury and not make assumptions. The following are some common assumptions friends and family make about those who self-injure:

- Assumption: "She's just looking for attention."

- Truth: While some people self-injure as a cry for help or to physically express what they are unable to communicate with words, most people go to great lengths to hide their behavior.

- Assumption: "She's being manipulative."

- Truth: For most people who self-injure, self-injuring is a private activity they keep hidden from others. Most people self-injure for the effect it has on them, not on others.

- Assumption: "He likes pain."

- Truth: Some people who self-injure do not feel pain. Others do. Everyone's pain threshold is different.

- Assumption: "He's trying to kill himself."

- Truth: People who self-injure are rarely trying to commit suicide. Some people who self-injure say it is a way they avert suicide by releasing the overwhelming or depressive feelings that build up inside.

- Assumption: "She's crazy. She'll hurt other people, too."

- Truth: People who self-injure are not crazy. Their violence is directed at themselves, not at others.

Seeking Treatment

The stress of constantly hiding self-injury can take an emotional toll. The behavior can take over a person's life and make him or her feel completely out of control. It is then the self-injurer may decide to seek outside help. But since self-injury is so often a private activity, it is usually a friend, a relative, or even a doctor doing a routine exam who discovers it.

Jennifer, a teen in a residential treatment program, was found cutting by a friend who told a counselor, who then notified Jennifer's parents. Jennifer resisted going to therapy until she realized she

REASONS TO STOP

According to the online self-injury support group Scar Tissue, the consequences of self-injury can come into focus when people who self-injure consider the following reasons for stopping:

- To not have to lie about how I'm feeling.
- To be normal again.
- To look at my parents and friends without shame.
- To not be a constant source of worry to those who love me.
- To not have to worry if tonight I'll mess up and hurt myself.
- To find my self-confidence and self-worth.
- To like the person I see in the mirror.
- To wear summer clothes without feeling self-conscious.[2]

was only hurting herself by not trying to get better: "I had to learn to let myself feel emotional pain and be OK with it," she told an interviewer. She also realized how important it was to ask for help: "Reaching out and talking to people who you're close with is absolutely the most helpful thing you can do to replace cutting."[3]

Whether a self-injurer seeks help on his or her own or through someone else, there is no diagnostic test solely for self-injury. A doctor or mental health provider will ask a number of questions as part of an evaluation. They will further explore any answers about self-injury and then make treatment recommendations.

Treatment Options

If someone is severely self-injuring, a doctor may recommend short-term hospitalization until the person is out of crisis. Some type of counseling therapy is then important to get to the root of the self-injurer's underlying problems—to understand and work through the uncomfortable feelings so the feelings do not come back. Counseling can help people become aware of what actions or events trigger episodes of self-injury and learn better coping skills so they can make healthier choices. Counseling can also help with self-esteem and any other

Counseling can help self-injurers understand their triggers and work to break their self-injuring habits.

mental health issues the self-injurer may be struggling with. Types of counseling therapy that have been used with self-injury patients include:

- Cognitive behavioral—This form of counseling trains people to become aware of their negative beliefs and behaviors. They are then taught how to replace their negative beliefs and behaviors with healthier choices.

- Psychodynamic—This form focuses on looking at and working through hidden memories and past issues at the root of current problems.

- Mindfulness—Mindfulness counseling focuses on the present moment. Patients are taught how to know what other people are really thinking and doing; the goal is to lower stress and improve general well-being.

- Dialectical behavioral therapy (DBT)—DBT counseling encourages self-acceptance while also promoting change. Self-injurers learn to see themselves as being in control of their lives, rather than as victims.

- Individual therapy, residential programs, and day treatment programs are all useful ways for getting appropriate therapy. Family therapy is often included as an important part of many treatment programs.

Self-Help and Coping

In addition to professional treatment, there are several things self-injurers can do to help with their own recovery:

- Call a chosen friend or family member when feeling the urge to self-injure.

- Take good care of wounds and get medical help if needed; ask a friend or relative for support.

- Do not share self-injury instruments, which can raise the risk of infection and disease.

- Be aware of situations and feelings that can trigger self-injury; when these situations come up, do something to distract yourself or call a chosen support person.

SELF-HELP DISTRACTION TECHNIQUES

Some self-injurers find relief in safe behaviors similar to the injuring activity, such as snapping a rubber band on the wrist, pressing ice to the skin, rubbing in lotion, or drawing a red line on the arm. Another self-help technique is switching to a different activity for a few minutes. Yoga, meditation, and reaching out to a friend are other methods people have used. The following are some additional activities people use when coping with the urge to self-injure:

- Hit a pillow, cushion, or punching bag to vent frustration and anger
- Scream into a pillow or cushion
- Go outdoors
- Run, walk, or do any kind of physical exercise
- Play a musical instrument, or simply make noise by banging pots and pans
- Dance
- Write negative emotions on a piece of paper and then rip it up
- Write in a journal
- Scribble with red crayons
- Make clay sculptures and smash them
- Flatten aluminum cans for recycling
- Break sticks

- Express emotions in positive ways by exercising, dancing, making art, or playing music.

- Stay away from alcohol and drugs, which can impair judgment and make self-injuring more likely.

- Seek out websites promoting recovery, but stay away from sites promoting self-injury.

- Seek help right away if feeling suicidal, such as by calling the National Suicide Prevention Lifeline 24-hour crisis line at 800-273-8255 (800-273-TALK).

Greater awareness of self-injury is a double-edged sword. While it can shine a bright light on a hidden behavior, it may also increase the chance a hurting teen will choose it as a way to cope. Given the feelings of isolation and low self-esteem shared by so many young people who self-injure, the solution is no easy task. At least when those who self-injure are ready to stop, help is available.

"I've learned that people appreciate me for who I am, and whether or not I'm cutting, I'm a valuable person. I still have a reason to be here."[4]
—Lila, a teen recovering from self-injury

Yoga can be a great outlet for self-injurers to express their emotions and release stress.

TIMELINE

Late 1800s
Psychotherapist Sigmund Freud theorizes
self-mutilation is a failed suicide attempt.

1938
The book *Man Against Himself* by physician Karl
Menninger is published. Menninger theorizes
self-injury is an attempt to avoid suicide by
sacrificing a small portion of the body.

1967
Psychiatrists Harold Graff and Richard Mallin publish
an article in July, describing a "wrist-cutting syndrome"
in which the sufferer does not try to commit suicide.

1979
English researcher Richard J. Turner renames
self-injurious behavior "non-fatal deliberate self-harm."

1983

Psychiatric researchers J. Kahan and E. M. Pattison publish a paper describing a "deliberate self-harm syndrome." In it, they theorize self-injury occurs as a result of problems with impulse control.

1985

S.A.F.E. Alternatives, the first inpatient treatment program designed specifically for self-injury, is founded.

1987

Cultural psychiatrist Armando Favazza's *Bodies Under Siege* is published, in which Favazza explores the idea that self-injury is partly an attempt at self-healing.

1992

Diana: Her True Story, a biography of Princess Diana by Andrew Morton, is published. Excerpts appear in *People* magazine, including her revelations about self-injury.

TIMELINE

1993

Actor Johnny Depp reveals in a magazine interview that he cut his arms. In the same year, the article "A Bright Red Scream" appears in the November issue of *San Francisco Focus* magazine, containing interviews with noncelebrities who self-injure.

1995

In November, Princess Diana explains in an interview on British television why she injures herself.

1998

Singer Fiona Apple admits to biting her lip and scratching herself in an interview with *Rolling Stone* magazine.

2008

Chicago radiologists discover ten teenage girls who had repeatedly inserted objects into their skin over the course of three years. Researchers coined the newly discovered self-injuring behavior "self-embedding disorder."

2010

A study published in the October issue of *Journal of Adolescent Health* shows there is a link between self-injury and eating disorders; also in October, singer Demi Lovato reveals on the MTV special *Stay Strong* that she self-injures.

2011

In February, research published in the journal *Pediatrics* shows cutting makes up 14 to 24 percent of the top YouTube videos.

2012

In February, Internet host-site Tumblr bans blogs glorifying self-injury.

2013

Nonsuicidal self-injury (NSSI) is added to the *Diagnostic and Statistical Manual of Mental Disorders (DSM-5)* in May.

ESSENTIAL FACTS

At Issue

- Self-injury is a growing trend. Approximately 1 percent of the total US population self-injures.

- Self-injury is a global issue. In 2013, the number of young people treated in UK hospitals for self-injury rose 11 percent compared with 2012. Hospital treatment for self-injury involving UK children ages 10 to 14 jumped 30 percent.

- Self-injury has short and long-term physical and emotional consequences, including physical scarring, damaged relationships, and an increased risk of suicide.

- Since 1994, self-injury has proliferated in the media and on the Internet. Critics say the attention spreads the practice. Others say the attention brings needed awareness to the secretive behavior.

- While 90 percent of those who self-injure stop on their own, 10 percent continue into adulthood, possibly because of unresolved mental health issues.

Critical Dates

1890s to 1970s

Sigmund Freud and his contemporaries deemed self-injury attempted suicide. Then researchers began noticing some women cutting their wrists were attempting to cope with emotional trauma. Because these women often had severe underlying emotional problems, the behavior was considered a symptom of mental disorders.

1980s and 1990s

Attitudes about self-injury changed in the 1980s and 1990s for a number of reasons: Respected and well-known celebrities, such as Princess Diana, revealed they self-injured; new research showed those who self-injured did not always have mental health disorders; and the media began publishing interviews with celebrities and noncelebrities who self-injured.

Late 1990s to present

Self-injury became somewhat of a fad as the Internet expanded and more celebrity revelations surfaced. Anyone curious about self-injury could find images, videos, and descriptions of the behavior on blogs, message boards, and other sites devoted to the topic. Self-injury appeared in movies, TV programs, and song lyrics, leading to what some mental health experts believe is an epidemic of self-injury.

Quote

"Self-mutilators seek what we all seek: an ordered life, spiritual peace—and maybe even salvation—and a healthy mind and body. Their desperate methods are upsetting to those of us who try to achieve these goals in a more tranquil manner, but the methods rest firmly on the dimly perceived bedrock of human experience."—*Armando Favazza, professor of psychiatry at the University of Missouri-Columbia, 1996*

GLOSSARY

amputation
The removal or cutting off of a body part.

anorexia nervosa
An eating disorder characterized by a fear of weight gain, resulting in deliberate malnourishment and excessive weight loss.

anxiety
An overwhelming feeling of worry, fear, or nervousness about what may happen.

autism
A mental condition with onset in childhood characterized by difficulty communicating and forming relationships.

bulimia
An eating disorder characterized by overeating and vomiting afterward in an attempt to avoid weight gain.

depression
A mental disorder marked by sadness, inactivity, loss of interest in usual activities, feelings of dejection and hopelessness, and some physical symptoms.

mutilation
An instance of injuring seriously by cutting, tearing, or breaking off some part.

parasuicidal
Apparent attempted suicide.

pathological
Extreme in an abnormal way.

stereotype
A widely held but simple idea, opinion, or image of a person or group.

stigma
A mark of shame or discredit.

syndrome
A group of symptoms that occur together.

ADDITIONAL RESOURCES

Selected Bibliography

Adler, Patricia A., and Peter Adler. *The Tender Cut: Inside the Hidden World of Self-Injury.* New York: New York UP, 2011. Print.

Favazza, Armando R. M.D. *Bodies Under Siege.* 2nd ed. Baltimore, MD: Johns Hopkins, 1996. Print.

Lundsten, Apryl. "Cutting Edge." *Girl's Life* 17:6 (July 2011). *EBSCO Host*. Web. 19 Oct. 2013.

Further Readings

Allman, Toney. *Self-Injury.* Detroit, MI: Lucent, 2011. Print.

Shapiro, Lawrence. *Stopping the Pain: A Workbook for Teens Who Cut and Self Injure.* Oakland, CA: New Harbinger, 2008. Print.

Williams, Mary E., ed. *Self-Injury.* Detroit, MI: Greenhaven, 2013. Print.

Websites

To learn more about Essential Issues, visit **booklinks.abdopublishing.com**. These links are routinely monitored and updated to provide the most current information available.

For More Information

For more information on this subject, contact or visit the following organizations:

S.A.F.E. Alternatives
800-366-8288
http://www.selfinjury.com
S.A.F.E. Alternatives is an inpatient center for self-injurers. Treatment is nonjudgmental, and patients are afforded the freedom to make healthy choices.

Self Injury Foundation
PO BOX 962
South Haven, MI 49090
888-962-NSSI (6774)
http://www.selfinjuryfoundation.org
The Self Injury Foundation provides support, education, and funding for self-injurers and self-injury research.

SOURCE NOTES

Chapter 1. Self-Injury: A Growing Trend

1. "Princess Diana Interview Part 2." *YouTube*. YouTube, 22 Oct. 2008. Web. 9 Oct. 2013.

2. Jeffrey Kluger. "The Cruelest Cut." *Time Magazine*. Time, 9 May 2005. Web. 7 Oct. 2013.

3. "Famous Self-Injurers." *Self-injury.net*. Self-injury.net, n.d. Web. 9 Oct. 2013.

4. Steven Levenkron. *Cutting: Understanding and Overcoming Self-Mutilation*. New York: Norton, 1998. Print. 25.

5. Vivian Pencz. "Breathing While Drowning: Youth Who Self-Harm." *Vivian Pencz*. WordPress, Dec. 2012. Web. 10 Oct. 2013.

6. Susan Seligson. "Cutting: The Self-Injury Puzzle." *BU Today*. Boston University, 4 Mar. 2013. Web. 6 Oct. 2013.

7. "Self-Injury." *Mental Health America*. Mental Health America, n.d. Web. 7 Oct. 2013.

8. Jason J. Washburn, et al. "Psychotherapeutic Approaches to Non-Suicidal Self-Injury in Adolescents." *Child and Adolescent Psychiatry and Mental Health*. BioMed Central, 2012. Web. 6 Oct. 2013.

9. Susan Seligson. "Cutting: The Self-Injury Puzzle." *BU Today*. Boston University, 4 Mar. 2013. Web. 6 Oct. 2013.

10. Jason J. Washburn, et al. "Psychotherapeutic Approaches to Non-Suicidal Self-Injury in Adolescents." *Child and Adolescent Psychiatry and Mental Health*. BioMed Central, 2012. Web. 6 Oct. 2013.

11. Susan Seligson. "Cutting: The Self-Injury Puzzle." *BU Today*. Boston University, 4 Mar. 2013. Web. 6 Oct. 2013.

12. "Self-Inflicted Injury Prevention, Children Ages 10 to 19 Years." *New York State Department of Health*. New York State, n.d. Web. 7 Oct. 2013.

13. Mary Peterson Kauffold. "Providing Help to Those on the Edge." *Chicago Tribune*. Chicago Tribune, 29 Sept. 1996. Web. 15 Oct. 2013.

Chapter 2. What Is Self-Injury?

1. Jarryd Willis. "Understanding Cutting and Bullycide." *HuffPost*. TheHuffingtonPost.com, 19 July 2013. Web. 28 Oct. 2013.

2. "Long-Term Effects of Self-Harm." *TheSite*. TheSite.org, 29 Oct. 2013. Web. 30 Oct. 2013.

3. Emily Ann Kramer. "Self-Injury: A School-Wide Response to a Growing Problem." *Adler Graduate School*. Adler Graduate School, May 2011. Web. 25 Oct. 2013.

4. Patricia A. Adler and Peter Adler. *The Tender Cut: Inside the Hidden World of Self-Injury*. New York: New York University Press, 2011. Print. 200–201.

5. Leslie Goldman. "Cut to the Core: Self-Injurers Add Damage to the Deep Wounds Within." *Chicago Tribune*. Chicago Tribune, 21 Oct. 2001. Web. 15 Oct. 2013.

Chapter 3. The History of Self-Injury

1. Armando R. Favazza. *Bodies Under Siege*. 2nd ed. Baltimore, MD: Johns Hopkins, 1996. Print. 251–252.

Chapter 4. Who Self-Injures and Why

1. Armando R. Favazza. *Bodies Under Siege*. 2nd ed. Baltimore, MD: Johns Hopkins, 1996. Print. 18, 240.

2. Jennifer Huget. "Kids Start Self-Harm Early." *Washington Post*. Washington Post, 6 Nov. 2011. Web. 15 Oct. 2013.

3. Patricia A. Adler and Peter Adler. *The Tender Cut: Inside the Hidden World of Self-Injury*. New York: New York UP, 2011. Print. 71.

4. Jane E. Brody. "The Growing Wave of Teenage Self-Injury." *New York Times*. New York Times, 6 May 2008. Web. 8 Oct. 2013.

5. Ibid.

6. Jason J. Washburn, et al. "Psychotherapeutic Approaches to Non-Suicidal Self-Injury in Adolescents." *Child and Adolescent Psychiatry and Mental Health*. BioMed Central, 2012. Web. 6 Oct. 2013.

7. Patricia A. Adler and Peter Adler. *The Tender Cut: Inside the Hidden World of Self-Injury*. New York: New York UP, 2011. Print. 78.

8. Shari Roan. "Borderline Personality Disorder Grows as Healthcare Concern." *Los Angeles Times*. Los Angeles Times, 7 Sept. 2009. Web. 17 Oct. 2013.

9. Patricia A. Adler and Peter Adler. *The Tender Cut: Inside the Hidden World of Self-Injury*. New York: New York UP, 2011. Print. 171.

Chapter 5. Consequences of Self-Injury

1. Apryl Lundsten. "Cutting Edge." *Girl's Life* 17:6 (July 2011). *EBSCO Host*. Web. 19 Oct. 2013.

2. Kathiann M. Kowalski. "Hurting to Feel Better." *Current Health* 31:2 (1 Oct. 2007). *EBSCO Host*. Web. 19 Oct. 2013.

3. Leslie Goldman. "Cut to the Core: Self-Injurers Add Damage to the Deep Wounds Within." *Chicago Tribune*. Chicago Tribune, 21 Oct. 2001. Web. 15 Oct. 2013.

4. "Long-Term Effects of Self-Harm." *TheSite*. TheSite.org, 29 Oct. 2013. Web. 30 Oct. 2013.

5. "Self-Harm and Suicidal Behaviours." *Headspace*. Headspace National Youth Mental Health Foundation, n.d. Web. 30 Oct. 2013.

6. Emese Csipke, et al. "Understanding Self-Harm." *SANE*. Sane.org.uk, 1 Nov. 2008. Web. 29 Oct. 2013.

7. Celia Richardson. "The Truth About Self-Harm." *Mental Health Foundation.* Mentalhealth.org.uk, 2006. Web. 26 Nov. 2013.

8. Vivian Pencz. "Breathing While Drowning: Youth Who Self-Harm." *Vivian Pencz.* WordPress, Dec. 2012. Web. 10 Oct. 2013.

Chapter 6. Self-Injury and Society

1. Hayden Cooper. "Social Media Becoming 'Barometer' for Self-Harm as Rates Rise." *ABC News.* ABC, 11 Sept. 2013. Web. 29 Oct. 2013.

2. The British Psychological Society and the Royal College of Psychiatrists. "Self-Harm: The NICE Guideline on Longer-Term Management." *National Collaborating Centre for Mental Health.* Nice.org, 2012. Web. 29 Oct. 2013.

3. Jennifer J. Muehlenkamp, et al. "International Prevalence of Adolescent Non-Suicidal Self-Injury and Deliberate Self-Harm." *Child and Adolescent Psychiatry and Mental Health.* BioMed Central, 30 Mar. 2012. Web. 29 Nov. 2013.

4. Kate Hilpern. "Why Do So Many Children Self-Harm?" *The Independent.* Independent.co.uk, 8 Oct. 2013. Web. 29 Oct. 2013.

5. "Self Harm Rise Among Young in Wales 'Alarming.'" *BBC News Wales.* BBC, 4 May 2011. Web. 29 Nov. 2013.

6. Jennifer J. Muehlenkamp, et al. "International Prevalence of Adolescent Non-Suicidal Self-Injury and Deliberate Self-Harm." *Child and Adolescent Psychiatry and Mental Health.* BioMed Central, 30 Mar. 2012. Web. 29 Nov. 2013.

7. Kim Carollo. "Double Whammy: Eating Disorders, Self-Injury Linked, According to Study." *ABC News.* ABC News Internet Ventures, 8 Oct. 2010. Web. 17 Oct. 2013.

8. Ibid.

9. "Famous Self-Injurers." *Self-injury.net.* Self-injury.net, n.d. Web. 9 Oct. 2013.

10. Chris Heath. "Fiona: The Caged Bird Sings." *Rolling Stone.* Rolling Stone, 22 Jan. 1998. Web. 9 Oct. 2013.

11. Marla Lehner. "Megan Fox Admits She Cut Herself." *People.* Time, 16 Sept. 2009. Web. 8 Oct. 2013.

12. Sarah Anne Hughes. "Demi Lovato Talks about Ongoing Battle with Eating Disorder, Self-Harm on Special 'Stay Strong' (video)." *Washington Post.* Washington Post, 3 July 2012. Web. 15 Oct. 2013.

13. Karen Thomas. "New Mom Angelina Jolie Rocks the 'Cradle of Life.'" *USA Today.* USA Today, 17 July 2003. Web. 8 Oct. 2013.

Chapter 7. Self-Injury and the Internet

1. Caitlin Dewey. "Self-Harm Blogs Pose Problems and Opportunities." *Washington Post.* Washington Post, 9 Sept. 2013. Web. 3 Oct. 2013.

2. Ibid.

3. Kate Lunau. "Teenagers Wired to Take Risks." *Maclean's Magazine.* 11 Apr. 2011. Web. 21 Oct. 2013.

4. Ibid.

5. Caitlin Dewey. "Self-Harm Blogs Pose Problems and Opportunities." *Washington Post*. Washington Post, 9 Sept. 2013. Web. 3 Oct. 2013.

6. Mary Forgione. "YouTube Cutting and Self-Injury Videos Draw Increasing Number of Viewers, Study Finds." *Los Angeles Times*. Los Angeles Times, 21 Feb. 2011. Web. 15 Oct. 2013.

7. Leslie Horn. "Tumblr Bans Blogs that Promote Self-Harm." *PC Magazine*. Ziff Davis, 23 Feb. 2012. Web. 17 Oct. 2013.

8. Apryl Lundsten. "Cutting Edge." *Girl's Life* 17:6 (July 2011). *EBSCO Host*. Web. 19 Oct. 2013.

9. Keith Ablow. "The Truth About YouTube Videos and Self-Injury." *FOX News*. FOX News Network, 22 Feb. 2011. Web. 15 Oct. 2013.

10. Apryl Lundsten. "Cutting Edge." *Girl's Life* 17:6 (July 2011). *EBSCO Host*. Web. 19 Oct. 2013.

11. Patricia A. Adler and Peter Adler. *The Tender Cut: Inside the Hidden World of Self-Injury.* New York: New York UP, 2011. Print. 165.

12. Nina Lincoff. "Childhood Bullying Is Tied to Adolescent Self-Harm." *Healthline*. Healthline Networks, 31 May 2013. Web. 29 Nov. 2013.

13. Kate Hilpern. "Why Do So Many Children Self-Harm?" *The Independent*. Independent.co.uk, 8 Oct. 2013. Web. 29 Oct. 2013.

Chapter 8. What's Being Done about Self-Injury?

1. Emily Ann Kramer. "Self-Injury: A School-Wide Response to a Growing Problem." *Adler Graduate School*. Adler Graduate School, May 2011. Web. 25 Oct. 2013.

2. Stephen Ceasar. "Glendale District Says Social Media Monitoring Is for Student Safety." *Los Angeles Times*. Los Angeles Times, 14 Sept. 2013. Web. 30 Oct. 2013.

3. Laura A. Dorko Mueller. "Common Reactions." *Educators and Self-Injury*. Laura A. Dorko Mueller, n.d. Web. 30 Oct. 2013.

4. Matthew D. Selekman. "Helping Self-Harming Students." *ASCD*. ASCD, Jan. 2010. Web. 23 Oct. 2013.

5. Petra Rattue. "Self-Harm Detected in Many Teenagers, Majority Stop by Adulthood." *MNT*. Medical News Today, 18 Nov. 2011. Web. 31 Oct. 2013.

Chapter 9. Treatment: Helping Those Who Self-Injure

1. Sarah Feuerbacher. Personal communications. 25 Nov. 2013.

2. "Reducing and Stopping Self Harm." *Scar-tissue.net*. Scar Tissue, n.d. Web. 29 Oct. 2013.

3. Apryl Lundsten. "Cutting Edge." *Girl's Life* 17:6 (July 2011). *EBSCO Host*. Web. 19 Oct. 2013.

4. Vivian Pencz. "Breathing While Drowning: Youth Who Self-Harm." *Vivian Pencz*. WordPress, Dec. 2012. Web. 10 Oct. 2013.

INDEX

ABOUT THE AUTHOR

Melissa Higgins writes fiction and nonfiction for children and young adults. Her novel for struggling readers, *Bi-Normal*, won the 2013 Independent Publisher (IPPY) silver-medal award for Young Adult Fiction. She has written more than 30 nonfiction titles on topics ranging from science and technology to history and biographies. While the wide array of topics reflects her varied interests, she especially enjoys writing about issues related to mental health. Before becoming a full-time writer, Higgins worked as a school counselor. When not writing, she enjoys hiking and taking photographs in the Arizona desert where she lives with her husband.

ABOUT THE CONSULTANT

Dr. Feuerbacher is a licensed clinical social worker supervisor, practical parent education certified parent educator, and state of Texas parent mediator and facilitator. Dr. Feuerbacher earned a bachelor's degree in social work, master of social work, and doctorate of philosophy in educational psychology from Baylor University. She is the current Center for Family Counseling clinic director and teaches in the Dispute Resolution and Counseling graduate department at Southern Methodist University. Dr. Feuerbacher's clinical and public speaking focus is in the areas of holistic approaches to creating healthy relationships and lifestyles by working with individuals who have experienced family abuse and/or self-injury.